Austin Dobson, Robert Herrick, Edwin Austin Abbey

Selections from the Poetry of Robert Herrick

Austin Dobson, Robert Herrick, Edwin Austin Abbey

Selections from the Poetry of Robert Herrick

ISBN/EAN: 9783337777814

Printed in Europe, USA, Canada, Australia, Japan

Cover: Foto ©Thomas Meinert / pixelio.de

More available books at **www.hansebooks.com**

TO ALFRED·PARSONS THE·DRAWINGS·IN· THIS·BOOK·ARE· ·DEDICATED AVG:1882·

E·A·A·

Contents

Chloris Walking in the Snow is taken from Wits Recreation of 1640. Grosart, in his edition of Herrick in 1876, rejects this poem, and states as his reason that there are no less than 62 pieces common to Wits Recreation and the Hesperides, and from this fact he believes that Herrick instructed his publisher to take the poems of his composition in Wits Recreation for the Hesperides, and that this was not copied denotes definitely that Herrick was not the writer of it.

B

Preface.

E rêve de la vie champêtre"—*as* Georges Sand *has said compactly in the delightful* Mare au Diable—"a été de tout temps l'idéal des villes." *Deny it as we may, we have all had, or must have it,—that fever of the fields. We may prate with Captain* Morris *of our shaded* Pall Mall ; *we may hug ourselves with* Lamb *on the " sweet security of streets"; we may romance at large upon the liberties of locomotion and the merits of the morning paper; but to each and all of us, the young, the old—and even the middle-aged—has come or will come, to-day or to-morrow, that hunger for the hills and woods,—that craving for country scenes and sights. Old places that we never noted, old things that we never re-member to have forgotten, flash suddenly "upon our inward eye," and crowd back "into our study of imagi-nation." Where was it that we saw those three little ducks huddling together in the sunlight, by what forgotten farm door, at whose porch a convolvulus climbed over a laurel?—where that shaggy and loose-limbed mare, whose foal lay rolling in the grass ? We never seem to have regarded that "cornfield-side a-flutter with poppies," and yet here they are, in black and scarlet, dancing like* Wordsworth's *daffodils. And where is that hedge of meadow-sweet and dog-rose, with the mower's jacket and stone-bottle and watch-ful terrier which lie so distinctly on our retina ? Old*

groups

i.

groups of cattle under trees whose shadows lengthen on the slopes; old dusty teams led tinkling to the water; little bridges by mills where the stream comes rushing blackly from sombre under-channels; gray quarries where the sand-martins have honey-combed the chalk; willowy hollows and restful river-banks where the "very fearful" chub lie unsuspecting at the surface; roofs rusted with lichen, and crested with house-leek, where processional pigeons "most do congregate"; cottages with their round wells, and homely door-settles, and honest garden-flowers— their marjoram, and peony, and pink, and marygold; all these troop back disorderly, confusedly, when we yield our- selves captive to the whim and the hour. As the vision is the more unreasonable, as the time is the more ill-timed, the more complete is our surrender. By and by, humanity, too, slips slowly into our ken. And at this stage we are conscious of a certain obliquity—a certain dishonesty—in our mental photography: it is not the "horn-handed breaker of the glebe," still less the agricultural labourer of the blue- books, who people our solitudes. It is the peasant of the artist, in his spotless smock and picturesque wideawake, with his apple-cheeked spouse and his white-haired children. Or it is that pastoral personage of the poets, who never lived but in the Nomansland *of* Arcadian *unreality where, as some one said, "peers of the realm pipe on rocks, in velvet panta- loons." It is "neat-handed* Phyllis" *with her savoury messes; it is winsome* Amaryllis; *it is* Thestylis *binding the sheaves with* Corydon *beside her; it is* Doris, *and* Chloris, *and* Lalage, *and the rest. We are deceived, and we wish to be so; we are the victims of an amiable insanity; we are stirred by that pristine* Pan *whose mark we have all of us somewhere about us, like the sharp ear-tip in the* Faun *of* Praxiteles. "Le rêve de la vie champêtre a été de tout temps l'idéal des villes."

In

In such a mingling of memory and fancy, in such a mood ungratified, there is no better companion than that old poet of the Seventeenth Century who wandered in his Devon *lanes at* May-time, *and sang, in " cleanly-wantonnesse " and golden-hearted words, of* Julia *and* Corinna. *With* Herrick *we become spectators of a country-life which time has " softly moulded in the filmy blue " of doubtfullest remoteness, and over which his poetry has cast its inalienable—its imperishable charm. With him we walk about our*

"owne dear bounds
Not envying others larger grounds"

and watch

"a present God-like Power
Imprinted in each Herbe and Flower :
And smell the breath of great-ey'd Kine,
Sweet as the blossomes of the Vine."

With him we behold the

"large sleek Neat
Unto the Dew-laps up in meat :"

or

"view the flocks
Of sheep, (safe from the Wolfe and Fox)
And find their bellies there as full
Of short sweet grasse, as backs with wool."

With him we eat " Tarts and Custards " at Wakes ; with him we linger at May-poles *and* Morris-dances, *at " Sheering-feasts " and* Mummeries, *at Hock-carts and " Barly-Breaks "; we revel with him at " Twelfe-tide " and "Christmas," and share the*

"Nut-browne mirth, the Russet wit,"

where

"no man payes too deare for it."

With him, lest coy maids should see goblins, we tear down the mistletoe and holly on Candlemas *eve ; and spread, at*

Whitsuntide,

iii.

Whitsuntide, *with green rushes and "sweetest Bents," the new adornéd house.* "When the Rose *raignes,"—when, (it may be), he has quaffed a health to* Ovid or Catullus, *and the*
"immensive cup
Of *Aromatike* wine"
has cast a classic haze over his English *eye-sight, we join our voices to his, and sing of kisses and "True-love knots," of "cherry lips" and*
"Cheeks like Creame Enclarited."
We sigh with him
"as Lovers do :
And talk of Brides ; & who shall make
This wedding-smock, this Bridal-Cake
That Dress, this Sprig, that Leaf, this Vine;
That smooth and silken Columbine.
This done, we draw lots, who shall buy
And guild the Baies and Rosemary :
What Posies for our Wedding Rings ;
What gloves we'l give, and Ribanings :
And smiling at our selves, decree,
Who then the joyning *Priest* shall be.
What short sweet Prayers shall be said ;
And how the Posset shall be made
With cream of Lillies (not of Kine)
And *Maiden's-blush*, for spiced wine."
We are never tired of hearing him sing of Julia's *dress and its "brave Vibration," of her "handsome Anger," of her "Lawnes" and "Tiffanies," her "haire fill'd with Dew" and her "Quarelets of Pearl." Nor is it any defect in this delightful lyrist that (as* Horace *before him) he sings with equal gust of* Dianemé *and* Perenna, *of* Electra *and* Anthea, *or of the three "dainty Destinies," who weave his "Armilet." And now again we take part in that fairy service of King* Oberon, *where stands*

"Just

iv.

"Just in the middle of the Altar
Upon an end, the *Fairie-Psalter*,,
Grac't with the Trout-flies curious wings";
and where
" Hard by, i'th'shell of halfe a nut,
The holy-water there is put";
or we assist at those pretty pagan hymnlets where he vows
"*Daffadills*" *to* Bacchus, *or a peacock to* Juno, *or a*
"*broad-fac't Owle*" *to* Minerva. *Or we listen to him when,*
in those divinest lines, he bids a bride come on,
" and yeeld
A savour like unto a blessed field,
When the bedabled Morne
Washes the golden eares of corne";
or prays to music to " *becalme his Fever,*"—*to*
" Fall on him like a silent dew,
Or like those Maiden showrs,
Which, by the peepe of day, doe strew
A Baptime o're the flowers."
But in the mood with which this paragraph began, it is chiefly
as the fresh singer of the country-life, that we prize and
praise him most. He fits our whim by his clear and lucid
vision of natural objects, and he peoples his landscapes with
figures that we would see, if we could, and know, if it might
be. He adds too that, which, without him, our unspeculative
eyes might seek in vain,—
" the light that never was, on sea or land,
The consecration, and the Poet's dream."
And here it is necessary to justify a certain air
of partiality in the series of poems to which these words
are prefatory. To find in Herrick *but the idyllic and the*
amorous,—to see in him no more than the bard of those
" unbaptized Rhimes
Writ in his wild unhallowed Times,"—
is

v.

is to forget (as it cannot but seem) his graver and austerer
Muse,—to lose in the apple-orchards of the Hesperides *the
vesper-chiming of the* Noble Numbers. *Such a forgetful-
ness, however,—such a profane misliking, is far from
those to whom this gathering is due. If they have forborne
to tread the dim aisles where* "*the pealing organ blows,*"
*and lingered rather among the deep grasses and zigzag
fruit-tree-arms,—if their motto has been rather* "leviore
plectro" *than* "*At a solemn Musick,*" *it is because ·their
humour has been more often gay than grave, and that it is
in their* "trop lasche oysifveté" *that they have read their*
Poet. *Hence, in this their garland, they make no claim
to have exhausted all the flower-beds. They do not pretend
to be representative, or eclectic, or chronological—or even
aesthetic! If any outline or vision of a plan may be said
to have affected them, it has been to lean somewhat to those
pieces which deal with the rustic pictures, the old-world
pleasures, the simple folk-lore of an earlier and less progress-
ridden* England. *But even to admit this, is to admit too much.
Such an anthology as might grow up in a painter's studio,
where, through some sunny afternoon, one reads aloud while
the other works, would be the fittest image of the present
selection. Suppose afterwards that the whole were printed
together—the pictures which were drawn, the poems which
were read, and the volume before the reader is sufficiently
explained. To explain it more fully or more precisely
would be to detain him needlessly—nay even discourteously,
from the dainties before him. For who but an Ancient
Mariner would button-hole a bidden guest where the host
is ROBERT HERRICK!*

Austin Dobson.

*W*HITHER *Mad maiden* wilt thou roame?
  Farre safer 'twere to stay at home :
  Where thou mayst sit, and piping please
The poore and private *Cottages*.
Since *Coats*, and *Hamlets*, best agree
With this thy meaner Minstralsie.
There with the Reed, thou mayst expresse
The Shepherds Fleecie happinesse :
And with thy *Eclogues* intermixe
Some smooth, and harmlesse *Beucolicks*.
There on a Hillock thou mayst sing
Unto a handsome Shephardling ;
Or to a Girle (that keeps the Neat)
With breath more sweet than Violet.
There, there, (perhaps) such Lines as These
May take the simple *Villages*.
But for the Court, the Country wit
Is despicable unto it.
Stay then at home, and doe not goe
Or flie abroad to seeke for woe.
Contempts in Courts and Cities dwell ;
No *Critick* haunts the Poore mans Cell.
Where thou mayst hear thine own Lines read
By no one tongue, there, censured.
That man's unwise will search for Ill,
And may prevent it, sitting still.

2

To his Muse

THE ARGUMENT OF HIS BOOK.

I Sing of *Brooks*, of *Bloffomes*, *Birds*, and *Bowers* :
Of *April*, *May*, of *June*, and *July*-Flowers.
I sing of *May-poles*, *Hock-carts*. *Waffails*, *Wakes*,
Of *Bride-grooms*, *Brides*, and of their *Bridall-cakes*.
I write of *Youth*, of *Love*, and have Acceffe
By these, to sing of cleanly-*Wantoneffe*.
I sing of *Dewes*, of *Raines*, and piece by piece
Of *Balme*, of *Oyle*, of *Spice*, and *Amber-Greece*.
I sing of *Times trans-shifting ;* and I write
How *Roses* first came *Red*, and *Lillies White*.
I write of *Groves*, of *Twilights*, and I sing
The Court of *Mab*, and of the *Fairie-King*.
I write of *Hell ;* I sing (and ever shall)
Of *Heaven*, and hope to have it after all.

5

A BUCOLICK or DISCOVRSE of NEATHERDS

1 Come blithefull Neatherds let vs lay
   A wage who the best shall play
   Of thee or I the roundelay
   That fits the busines of the daye

Bor. And Iallage the Ivage shall be
      To giue the prize to thee, or me

2 Content, begin and I will bet
   A Heifer smooth, and black as jet
   In euery part alike compleat
   And wanton as a Kid as yet

A BEUCOLICK,
OR DISCOURSE OF NEATHERDS.

1 COME blithefull Neatherds, let us lay
    A wager, who the best shall play,
    Of thee, or I, the Roundelay,
That fits the businesse of the Day.

Chor. And *Lallage* the Judge shall be,
    To give the prize to thee, or me.

2 Content, begin, and I will bet
    A Heifer smooth, and black as jet,
    In every part alike compleat,
    And wanton as a Kid as yet.

Chor. And *Lallage* (with cow-like eyes)
    Shall be Disposeresse of the prize.

1 Against thy Heifer, I will here
    Lay to thy stake a lustie Steere,
    With gilded hornes, and burnisht cleere.
Chor. Why then begin, and let us heare
    The soft, the sweet, the mellow note
    That gently purles from eithers Oat.

2 The stakes are laid : let's now apply
    Each one to make his melody :
Lal. The equall Umpire shall be I,
    Who'l hear, and so judge righteously.

Chor. Much time is spent in prate ; begin,
    And sooner play, the sooner win.

                                         [He playes.

1 That's sweetly touch't, I must confesse :
   Thou art a man of worthinesse :
   But hark how I can now expresse
   My love unto my Neatherdesse.

Chor.   A suger'd note ! and sound as sweet
          As Kine, when they at milking meet.

4 Now for to win thy Heifer faire,
   I'le strike thee such a nimble Ayre,
   That thou shalt say (thy selfe) 'tis rare ;
   And title me without compare.

Chor.   Lay by a while your Pipes, and rest,
          Since both have here deserved best.

2 To get thy Steerling, once again,
   I'le play thee such another strain ;
   That thou shalt swear, my Pipe do's raigne
   Over thine Oat, as Soveraigne.

Chor.   And *Lallage* shall tell by this,
          Whose now the prize and wager is.

1 Give me the prize :   2. The day is mine :
1 Not so ; my Pipe has silenc't thine :
   And hadst thou wager'd twenty Kine,
   They were mine own.   *Lal.* In love combine.

Chor.   And lay we down our Pipes together,
          As wearie, not o'recome by either.

Cho*r*. *And Lallage, with cowlike eyes,*
Shall be difpoferefs of the prize.

Againfl thy Heifer I will heare
Lay to thy flake a lvftie fteere
With gilded horns and bvrnifhed cleere.

Chor. Why then begin, and let us heare
The soft, the sweet, the mellow note
That gently purles from either's oat.

1. The stakes are laid: let's now applie
Each one to make hys melodie.

Lal. The equall umpire shall be I
Who'll heare and so judge righteously

Chor. Much time is spent in prate; begin
And sooner play, the sooner win.
[He player

1   That's fweetly tovch'e I muft confeffe
Thou art a manne of worthleffe;
But hark how I can now expreffe
My lvue vnto my Neatherdeffe   [he fings

Chor.   A fvgard note! and found as fweete
      As Kine when they at milkinge meet

1   Nowe for to win thy Heifer faire
Ile ftrike mee fvch a nimble aire
That they fhalt faye thyfelfe, 'tis rare;
And title me without compare

Chor. Laye by awhile yovr pipes & reft
     Since both have heare deferved the beft

2   To get thy ferrling, once again
Ile play thee fvch another ftrain
That thou fhalt fwear my pipe do's raigne
Over thine eat as Soueraigne

Chor. And Lallage fhall tell by this
     whofe nowe the prize and wager is

1 Give me the prize:
2 The daye is mine:
3 Not so; my pipe has silenc'd thine:
   And hadst thou wager'd twenty Kine
   They were mine own
LxI. In Iuue combine

Chor. And lay we down our pipes together
      So wearie not o'ercome by either

TO BLOSSOEMS.

*F*CAIRE pledges of a fruitfull Tree,
  Why do yee fall so fast ?
  Your date is not so past ;
But you may stay yet here a while,
      To blush and gently smile ;
        And go at last.

What, were yee borne to be
      An houre or halfs delight ;
      And so to bid goodnight ?
Twas pitie Nature brought yee forth
      Meerly to shew your worth,
        And lose you quite.

But you are lovely Leaves, where we
      May read how soon things have
      Their end, though ne'r so brave :
And after they have shown their pride,
      Like you a while : They glide
        Into the Grave.

TO ANTHEA, WHO MAY COMMAND HIM ANY THING.

*B*ID me live, and I will live
  Thy Protestant to be ;
Or bid me love, and I will give
  A loving heart to thee.

A heart as soft, a heart as kind,
  A heart as sound and free,
As in the whole world thou canst find,
  That heart Ile give to thee.

Bid that heart stay, and it will stay,
  To honour thy Decree :
Or bid it languish quite away,
  And't shall doe so for thee.

Bid me to weep, and I will weep,
  While I have eyes to see :
And having none, yet I will keep
  A heart to weep for thee.

Bid me despaire, and Ile despaire,
  Under that *Cypresse* tree :
Or bid me die, and I will dare
  E'en Death, to die for thee.

Thou art my life, my love, my heart,
  The very eyes of me :
And hast command of every part,
  To live and die for thee.

A SHORT HYMNE TO VENVS

Goddesse, I do loue a girle
Rvbie-lipt and tooth'd with pearle.
If so be I may bvt proue
Lvckie in this Maide I loue,
I will promise there shall be
Mirtles offer'd vp to thee.

TO DAFFADILLS.

AIRE Daffadills, we weep to see
You haste away so soone :
As yet the early-rising Sun
Has not attain'd his Noone.
              Stay, stay,
Until the hasting day
              Has run
But to the Even-song ;
And, having pray'd together, we
Will goe with you along.

We have short time to stay, as you,
We have as short a Spring ;
As quick a growth to meet Decay,
As you, or any thing.
              We die,
As your hours doe, and drie
              Away,
Like to the Summers raine ;
Or as the pearles of Mornings dew
Ne'r to be found againe.

LOVE WHAT IT IS.

L OVE is a circle that doth restlesse move
In the same sweet eternity of love.

2   23

A Sweet disorder in the dresse
        Kindles in cloathes a wantonnesse :
        A Lawne about the shoulders thrown
Into a fine distraction :
An erring Lace, which here and there
Enthralls the Crimson Stomacher :
A Cuffe neglectfull, and thereby
Ribbands to flow confusedly :
A winning wave (deserving Note)
In the tempestuous petticote :
A carelesse shooe-string, in whose tye
I see a wilde civility :
Doe more bewitch me, then when Art
Is too precise in every part.

A SHORT HYMNE TO VENUS.

G ODDESSE, I do love a Girle
        Rubie-lipt, and tooth'd with *Pearl* :
        If so be, I may but prove
Luckie in this Maide I love :
I will promise there shall be
Mirtles offer'd up to Thee.

NO MAN WITHOUT MONEY.

N O man such rare parts hath, that he can swim,
        If favour or occasion helpe not him.

24

Delight in Disorder.

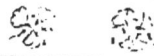

HIS CONTENT IN THE COUNTRY.

*H*ERE, here I live with what my Board,
    Can with the smallest cost afford.
    Though ne'r so mean the Viands be,
They well content my *Prew* and me.
Or Pea, or Bean, or Wort, or Beet,
What ever comes, content makes sweet :
Here we rejoyce, because no Rent
We pay for our poore Tenement :
Wherein we rest, and never feare
The Landlord, or the Usurer.
The Quarter-day do's ne'r affright
Our Peacefull slumbers in the night.
We eate our own, and batten more,
Because we feed on no mans score :
But pitie those, whose flanks grow great,
Swel'd with the Lard of others meat.
We blesse our Fortunes, when we see
Our own beloved privacie :
And like our living, where w'are known
To very few, or else to none.

UPON PARSON BEANES.

OLD Parson *Beanes* hunts six dayes of the week,
And on the seaventh, he has his Notes to seek.
Six dayes he hollows so much breath away,
That on the seaventh, he can nor preach, or pray.

TO A BED OF TULIPS.

BRIGHT Tulips, we do know,
You had your comming hither ;
And Fading-time do's show,
That Ye must quickly wither.

Your *Sister-hoods* may stay,
And smile here for your houre ;
But dye ye must away :
Even as the meanest Flower.

Come Virgins then, and see
Your frailties ; and bemone ye ;
For lost like these, 'twill be,
As Time had never known ye.

UPON A VIRGIN KISSING A ROSE.

TWAS but a single *Rose*,
Till you on it did breathe ;
But since (me thinks) it shows
Not so much *Rose*, as Wreathe.

23

UPON·A·VIRGIN·KISSING·
A·ROSE

Twas but a single Rose,
Till You on It did Breathe,
But since, Me thinks, it show
Not so much Rose as
Wreathe
R·Herrick.

DISCONTENTS IN DEVON.

*M*ORE discontents I never had
      Since I was born, then here ;
      Where I have been, and still am sad,
        In this dull *Devon-shire :*
Yet justly too I must confesse ;
   I ne'r invented such
Ennobled numbers for the Presse,
   Then where I loath'd so much.

HIS RETURNE TO LONDON.

*F*ROM the dull confines of the drooping West,
    To see the day spring from the pregnant East,
    Ravisht in spirit, I come, nay more, I flie
To thee, blest place of my Nativitie !
Thus, thus with hallowed foot I touch the ground,
                        With

31

With thousand blessings by thy Fortune crown'd.
O fruitful Genius ! that bestowes there
An everlasting plenty, yeere by yeere.
O *Place !* O *People !* Manners ! fram'd to please
All *Nations, Customes, Kindreds, Languages !*
I am a free-born *Roman ;* suffer then,
That I amongst you live a Citizen.
London my home is : though by hard fate sent
Into a long and irksome banishment ;
Yet since cal'd back ; henceforward let me be,
O native countrey, repossest by thee !
For, rather then I'le to the West return,
I'le beg of thee first here to have mine Urn ;
Weak I am grown, and must in short time fall ;
Give thou my sacred Reliques Buriall.

ALL THINGS DECAY AND DIE.

*A*LL *things decay with Time :* The Forrest sees
    The growth, and down-fall of her aged trees :
    That Timber tall, which three-score *lusters* stood
The proud *Dictator* of the State-like wood :
I meane (the Soveraigne of all Plants) the Oke
Droops, dies, and falls without the cleavers stroke.

TO DIANEME.

*D*EARE, though to part it be a Hell,
    Yet *Dianeme* now farewell :
    Thy frown (last night) did bid me goe ;
But whither, onely Grief do's know.

I

Vpon Ivlia's Clothes

When as in silks my Iulia goes,
Then, then (me thinks) how sweetly flowes
That liquefaction of her clothes.

Next, when I cast mine eyes and see
That brave vibration each way free
O how that Glittering taketh me!

Rob. Herrick

I doe beseech thee, ere we part,
(If mercifull, as faire thou art ;
Or else desir'st that Maids sho'd tell
Thy pitty by Loves-Chronicle)
O *Dianeme*, rather kill
Me, then to make me languish stil !
'Tis cruelty in thee to'th'height,
Thus, thus to wound, not kill out-right :
Yet there's a way found (if thou please)
By sudden death to give me ease :
And thus devis'd, doe thou but this,
Bequeath to me one parting kisse :
So sup'rabundant joy shall be
The Executioner of me.

HIS GRANGE, OR PRIVATE WEALTH

THOUGH Clock,
To tell how night drawes hence, I've none,
      A Cock,
I have, to sing how day drawes on.
      I have
A maid (my *Prew*) by good luck sent,
      To save
That little, Fates me gave or lent.
      A Hen
I keep, which creeking day by day,
      Tells when
She goes her long white egg to lay.
      A goose
I have, which, with a jealous care,
      Lets loose
         Her

33

Her tongue, to tell what danger's neare.

          A Lamb
I keep (tame) with my morsells fed,

          Whose Dam
An Orphan left him (lately dead.)

          A Cat
I keep, that playes about my House,

          Grown fat,
With eating many a miching Mouse

          To these
A *Trasy I do keep, whereby   *His Spaniel.

          I please
The more my rurall privacie :

          Which are
But toyes, to give my heart some ease :

          Where care
None is, slight things do lightly please.

POSTING TO PRINTING.

LET others to the Printing Presse run fast,
   Since after death comes glory, *Ile not haste.*

UPON JULIAS CLOTHES.

WHEN as in silks my *Julia* goes,
   Then, then (me thinks) how sweetly flowes
   That liquefaction of her clothes.
Next, when I cast mine eyes and see
That brave Vibration each way free ;
O how that glittering taketh me !

34

DIVINATION BY A DAFFADILL

WHEN a Daffadill I see,
    Hanging down his head t'wards me;
    Guesse I may, what I must be :
First, I shall decline my head ;
Secondly, I shall be dead ;
Lastly, safely buryed.

THE CRUELL MAID.

AND Cruell Maid, because I see
    You scornfull of my love, and me:
    Ile trouble you no more ; but goe
My way, where you shall never know
What is become of me : there I
Will find me out a path to die ;
Or learne some way how to forget
You, and your name, for ever : yet
Ere I go hence ; know this from me,
What will, in time, your Fortune be :
This to your coynesse I will tell ;
And having spoke it once, Farewell.

                       The

The Lillie will not long endure ;
Nor the Snow continue pure :
The Rose, the Violet, one day
See, both these Lady-flowers decay :
And you must fade, as well as they.
And it may chance that Love may turn,
And (like to mine) make your heart burn
And weep to see't ; yet this thing doe,
That my last Vow commends to you :
When you shall see that I am dead,
For pitty let a teare be shed ;
And (with your Mantle o're me cast)
Give my cold lips a kisse at last :
If twice you kisse, you need not feare,
That I shall stir, or live more here.
Next, hollow out a Tombe to cover
Me ; me, the most despised Lover :
And write thereon, *This, Reader, know,*
Love kill'd this man.   No more but so.

UPON CLUNN.

A Rowle of Parchment *Clunn* about him beares,
Charg'd with the Armes of all his Ancestors :
And seems halfe ravisht, when he looks upon
That *Bar*, this *Bend ;* that *Fess*, this Cheveron ;
This *Manch*, that *Moone ;* this *Martlet*, and that *Mound ;*
This counterchange of *Perle* and *Diamond.*
What joy can *Clun* have in that Coat, or this,
When as his owne still out at elboes is ?

Vpon Clvnn

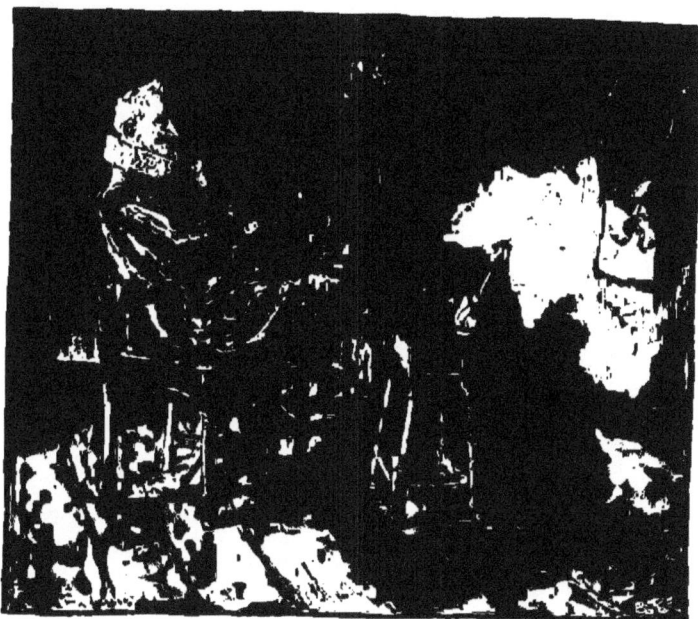

A rowle of parchment Clvnn aboue him beares,
Charg'd with the armes of all his ancestors:
And seems halfe rauisht, when he lookes vpon
That bar, this bend; that fess, this cheueron;
This manch, that mounts; this martlet, and that mound,
This counterchange of perle and diamond,
What ys can Clvnn haue in that coat, or this,
When as hys owne still out at elbows is?

THE BLEEDING HAND; OR, THE SPRIG OF EGLANTINE GIVEN TO A MAID

*F*ROM this bleeding hand of mine,
   Take this sprig of *Eglantine.*
   Which (though sweet unto your smell)
Yet the fretfull bryar will tell,
He who plucks the sweets shall prove
Many thorns to be in Love.

HIS PROTESTATION TO PERILLA.

*N*OONE-DAY and Midnight shall at once be seene:
   Trees, at one time, shall be both sere and greene:
   Fire and water shall together lye
In one-self-sweet-conspiring sympathie :
Summer and Winter shall at one time show
Ripe eares of corne, and up to th'eares in snow :
Seas shall be landlesse ; Fields devoid of grasse ;
Shapelesse the world, (as when all *Chaos* was)
Before, my deare *Perilla*, I will be
False to my vow, or fall away from thee.

GATHER ye Rose-buds while ye may,
    Old Time is still a flying :
And this same flower that smiles to day,
    To morrow will be dying.

The glorious Lamp of Heaven, the Sun,
    The higher he's a getting ;
The sooner will his Race be run,
    And neerer he's to Setting.

That Age is best, which is the first,
    When Youth and Blood are warmer;
But being spent, the worse, and worst
    Times, still succeed the former.

Then be not coy, but use your time ;
    And while ye may, goe marry :
For having lost but once your prime,
    You may for ever tarry.

UPON SAPHO, SWEETLY PLAYING, AND SWEETLY SINGING.

WHEN thou do'st play, and sweetly sing,
    Whether it be the voice or string,
    Or both of them, that do agree
Thus to en-trance and ravish me :
This, this I know, I'm oft struck mute ;
And dye away upon thy Lute.

VPON · SAPPHO

SWEETLY · PLAIE

INGE · AND ·

SWEETLY · SINGING ·

When thou dost play & sweetly sing
Whether it be the voice or string,
Or both of them, that do agree
Thus to entrance and ravish me;
This this I know, I'm oft struck mute
And dye away vpon thy lvte.

WHEN I thy singing next shall heare,
Ile wish I might turne all to eare,
To drink in Notes, and Numbers ; such
As blessed soules cann't heare too much :
Then melted down, there let me lye
Entranc'd, and lost confusedly :
And by thy Musique strucken mute,
Die, and be turn'd into a Lute.

A RING PRESENTED TO JULIA.

JULIA, I bring
To thee this Ring,
Made for thy finger fit ;
To shew by this,
That our love is
(Or sho'd be) like to it.

Close though it be,
The joynt is free :
So when Love's yoke is on,
It must not gall,
Or fret at all
With hard oppression.

But it must play
Still either way :
And be, too, such a yoke,
As not too wide,
To over-slide ;
Or be so strait to choak.

So

So we, who beare,
This beame, must reare
Our selves to such a height :
As that the stay
Of either may
Create the burden light.

And as this round
Is no where found
To flaw, or else to sever :
So let our love
As endless prove ;
And pure as Gold for ever.

THE TINKERS SONG.

ALONG, come along,
    Let's meet in a throng
        Here of Tinkers ;
And quaffe up a Bowle
As big as a Cowle
    To Beer Drinkers.
The pole of the Hop
Place in the Ale-shop
    to Bethwack us ;
If ever we think
So much as to drink
    Unto *Bacchus.*
Who frolick will be,
For little cost he
    Must not vary,
From Beer-broth at all,
So much as to call
    For Canary.

Along, come along,
Lets meet in a throng
    Here of tinkers
And quaffe up a bowle
As big as a cowle
    To beer drinkers

THE TINKERS SONG

The pole of the hop
Place in the ale-shop
    To bethwack us
If euer we think
So much as to drink
    Vnto Bacchus

Who frolick will be
For little cost he
    Must not vary
From beer-broth at all
So much as to call
    For canary.

R. Herricke.

THE SUCCESSION OF THE FOURE SWEET MONTHS.

*F*IRST, *April,* she with mellow showrs
Opens the way for early flowers ;
Then after her comes smiling *May,*
In a more rich and sweet aray :
Next enters *June,* and brings us more
Jems, then those two, that went before :
Then (lastly) *July* comes, and she
More wealth brings in, then all those three.

THE ROCK OF RUBIES: AND THE QUARRIE OF PEARLS.

*S*OME ask'd me where the *Rubies* grew ?
And nothing I did say :
But with my finger pointed to
The lips of *Julia.*
Some ask'd how *Pearls* did grow, and where ?
Then spoke I to my Girle,
To part her lips, and shew'd them there
The Quarelets of Pearl.

MONEY MAKES THE MIRTH.

*W*HEN all Birds els do of their musick faile
Money's the still-sweet-singing *Nightingale.*

49

*T*HE Hag is astride,
This night for to ride ;
The Devill and shee together :
Through thick, and through thin,
Now out, and then in,
Though ne'er so foule be the weather.

A Thorn or a Burr
She takes for a Spurre :
With a lash of a Bramble she rides now,
Through Brakes and through Bryars,
O're Ditches, and Mires,
She followes the Spirit that guides now.

No Beast, for his food,
Dares now range the wood ;
But husht in his laire he lies lurking :
While mischiefs, by these,
On Land and on Seas,
At noone of Night are a working,

The storme will arise,
And trouble the skies ;
This night, and more for the wonder,
The ghost from the Tomb
Affrighted shall come,
Cal'd out by the clap of the Thunder.

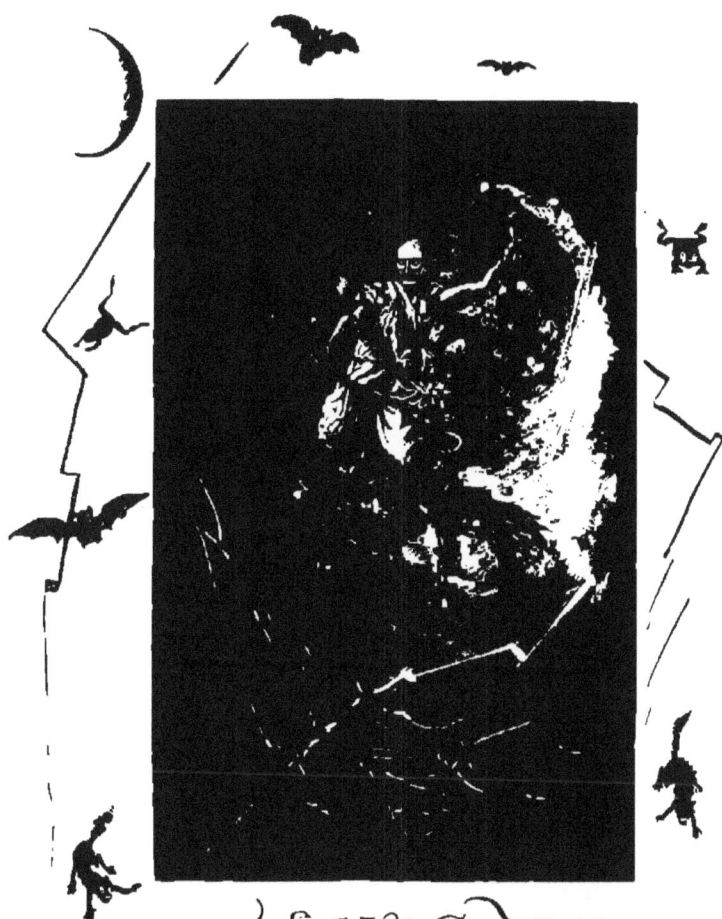

Ỹ HAG

Ỹ Hag is Astride
This Night for to Ride
Ỹ Deuill & Shee together.
Through Thick & Through Thin
Now Out & then In
Though ne'r so Fovle be ỹ Weather

A Thorn or a Burr
Shee takes for a Spvrre
With a Lash of a Bramble She Rides now
Through Brakes & through Bryars
O'er Ditches & Mires
Shee followes ỹ Spirit that Gvides now

No Beast for his food
Dares now range ỹ wood
But Hvsht in his laire he Lies Lvrking
While Mischiefs by these
On Land & on Seas
At Noone of Night are a Working

Ỹ Storme will arise
And Trovbles ỹ Skies
This Night & more for ỹ Wonder
Ỹ Ghost from ỹ Tomb
Affrighted shall come
Call'd out by ỹ Clap of ỹ Thvn

SHUT not so soon ; the dull-ey'd night
    Ha's not as yet begunne
    To make a seisure on the light,
    Or to seale up the Sun.

No Marigolds yet closed are ;
    No shadowes great appeare ;
Nor doth the early Shepheards Starre
    Shine like a spangle here.

Stay but till my *Julia* close
    Her life-begetting eye ;
And let the whole world then dispose
    It selfe to live or dye.

*F*LED are the Frosts, and now the Fields appeare
   Re-cloth'd in fresh and verdant Diaper.
   Thaw'd are the snowes, and now the lusty Spring
Gives to each Mead a neat enameling.
The Palms put forth their Gemmes, and every Tree
Now swaggers in her Leavy gallantry.
The while the *Daulian Minstrell* sweetly sings,
With warbling Notes, her Tyrrean sufferings.
What gentle Winds perspire ? As if here
Never had been the *Northern-Plunderer*
To strip the Trees, and Fields, to their distresse,
Leaving them to a pittied nakednesse.
And look how when a frantick Storme doth tear
A stubborn Oake, or Holme (long growing there)
But lul'd to calmnesse, then succeeds a breeze
That scarcely stirs the nodding leaves of Trees :
So when this War (which tempest-like doth spoil
Our salt, our Corn, our Honie, Wine, and Oile)
Falls to a temper, and doth mildly cast
His inconsiderate Frenzie off (at last)
The gentle Dove may, when these turmoils cease,
Bring in her Bill, once more, *the Branch of Peace.*

TO MEDDOWES

*Y*E have been fresh and green,
   Ye have been fill'd with flowers :
  And ye the Walks have been
   Where maids have spent their houres.
                     You

To Meadows

Ye have been fresh and green,
Ye have been fill'd with flowers;
And ye the walks have been
Where maids have spent their houres.

Ye have beheld, how they
With wicker arks did come
To kiss, and beare away
The richer cowslips home.

Y'ave heard them sweetly sing,
And seen them in a round:
Each virgin, like a spring,
With hony-succles crown'd.

But now, we see none here,
Whose silv'rie feet did tread,
And with dishevell'd haire,
Adorn'd this smoother mead.

Like unthrifts, having spent
Your stock, and needy grown,
Y'are left here to lament
Your poore estates, alone.

You have beheld, how they
  With *Wicker cArks* did come
To kisse, and beare away
  The richer Couslips home.

Y'ave heard them sweetly sing,
  And see them in a Round :
Each Virgin, like a Spring,
  With Hony-succles crown'd.

But now, we see, none here,
  Whose silv'rie feet did tread,
And with dishevell'd Haire,
  Adorn'd this smoother Mead.

Like Unthrifts, having spent,
  Your stock, and needy gown,
Y'are left here to lament
  Your poore estates, alone.

TO THE ROSE. SONG.

GOE happy Rose, and enterwove
  With other Flowers, bind my Love.
    Tell her too, she must not be,
Longer flowing, longer free,
That so oft has fetter'd me.

Say (if she's fretfull) I have bands
Of Pearle, and Gold, to bind her hands :
  Tell her, if she struggle still,
  I have Mirtle rods, (at will)
  For to tame, though not to kill.

                                        Take

57

Take thou my blessing, thus, and goe,
And tell her this, but doe not so,
   Lest a handsome anger flye,
   Like a Lightning, from her eye,
   And burn thee'up, as well as I.

TO THE WESTERN WIND.

SWEET Western Wind, whose luck it is,
   (Made rivall with the aire)
   To give *Perenna's* lip a kisse,
   And fan her wanton haire.

Bring me but one, Ile promise thee,
   Instead of common showers,
Thy wings shall be embalm'd by me,
   And all beset with flowers.

HIS CAVALIER.

GIVE me that man, that dares bestride
   The active Sea-horse, & with pride,
   Through that hugh field of waters ride:
Who, with his looks too, can appease
The ruffling winds and raging Seas,
In mid'st of all their outrages.
This, this a virtuous man can doe,
Saile against Rocks, and split them too ;
I ! and a world of Pikes passe through.

His Cavalier

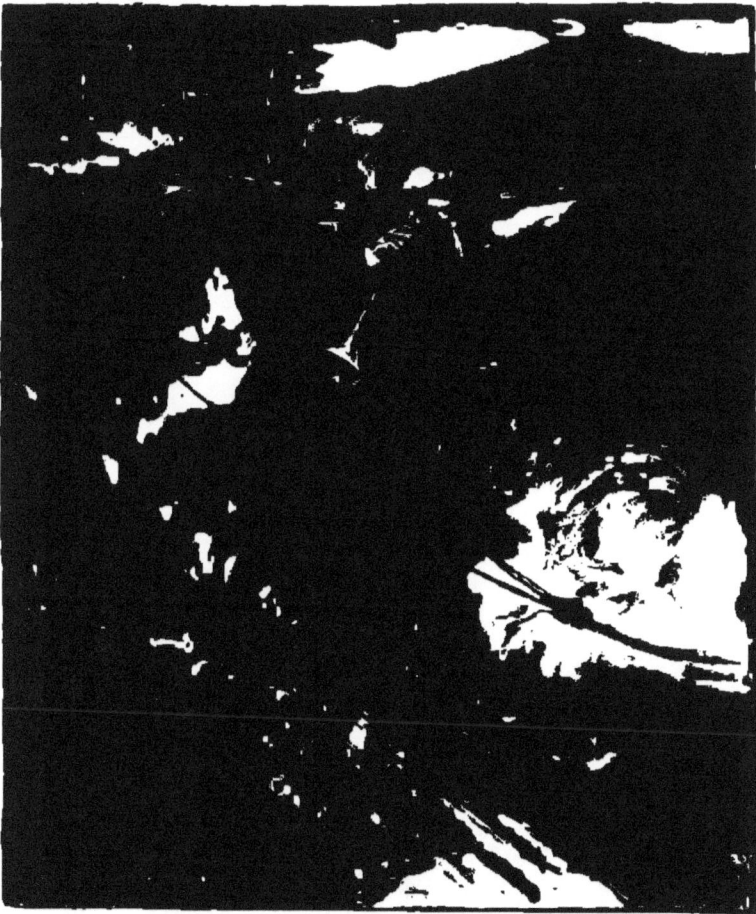

Giue me that Man, that dares bestride
The actiue Sea-horse & with pride
Throvgh that hvge field of waters ride:
Who, with his lookr too can appease
The rvffling winds and raging seas
In midst of all their Ovtrage;
This, this a uirtvovs Man can doe
Saile againft Rockr, and split them too;
I! and a World of pikes passe throvgh.

CEREMONIES FOR CHRISTMASSE.

COME, bring with a noise,
    My merrie merrie boyes,
The Christmas Log to the firing ;
    While my good Dame, she,
    Bids ye all be free ;
And drink to your hearts desiring.

    With the last yeeres brand
    Light the new block, And
For good successe in his spending,
    On your Psaltries play,
    That sweet luck may
Come while the Log is a teending.

    Drink now the strong Beere,
    Cut the white loafe here,
The while the meat is a shredding ;
    For the rare Mince-Pie
    And the Plums stand by
To fill the Paste that's a kneading.

THE CEREMONIES FOR CANDLEMASSE DAY.

KINDLE the Christmas Brand and then
        Till Sunne-set, let it burne ;
        Which quencht, then lay it up agen,
        Till Christmas next returne.

Part must be kept wherewith to teend
    The Christmas Log next yeare ;
And where 'tis safely kept, the Fiend,
    Can do no mischiefe (there.)

ONELY a little more
    I have to write,
        Then Ile give o're,
And bid the world Good-night.

'Tis but a flying minute,
    That I must stay,
        Or linger in it ;
And then I must away.

O time that cut'st down all !
    And scarce leav'st here
        Memoriall
Of any men that were.

How many lye forgot
    In Vaults beneath ?
        And piece-meale rot
Without a fame in death ?

Behold this living stone,
    I reare for me,
        Ne'r to be thrown
Downe, envious Time by thee.

Pillars let some set up,
    (If so they please)
        Here is my hope,
And my *Pyramides.*

His Poetrie his Pillar

Onely a little more
I have to write
Then I'll giue o'er
And bid the world goodnight.

'Tis but a flying minute
That I must stay
Or linger in it
And then I must away

O Time that cut'st down all
And scarce leav'st here
Memoriall
Of any men that were

How many lye forgot
In vaults beneath
And piecemeale rot
Without a fame in death.

Behold this liuing stone
I reare for me.
Ne'r to be thrown
Downe envious Time, by thee,

Pillars let some set vp·
If so they please
Here is my hope
And my pyramid's

A TERNARIE OF LITTLES, UPON A PIPKIN OF JELLIE SENT TO A LADY.

A Little Saint best fits a little Shrine,
A little prop best fits a little Vine,
As my small Cruse best fits my little Wine.

A little Seed best fits a little Soyle,
A little Trade best fits a little Toyle :
As my small Jarre best fits my little Oyle.

A little Bin best fits a little Bread,
A little Garland fits a little Head :
As my small stuffe best fits my little Shed.

A little Hearth best fits a little Fire,
A little Chappell fits a little Quire,
As my small Bell best fits my little Spire.

A little streame best fits a little Boat ;
A little lead best fits a little Float ;
As my small Pipe best fits my little note.

A little meat best fits a little bellie,
As sweetly Lady, give me leave to tell ye,
This little Pipkin fits this little Jellie.

A MEDITATION FOR HIS MISTRESSE.

Y OU are a *Tulip* seen to day,
But (Dearest) of so short a stay ;
That where you grew, scarce man can say.

You

65

You are a lovely *July-flower*,
Yet one rude wind, or ruffling shower,
Will force you hence, (and in an houre.)

You are a sparkling *Rose* i'th'bud,
Yet lost, ere that chast flesh and blood
Can shew where you or grew, or stood.

You are a full-spread faire-set Vine,
And can with Tendrills love intwine,
Yet dry'd, ere you distill your Wine.

You are like Balme inclosed (well)
In *Amber*, or some *Chrystall* shell,
Yet lost ere you transfuse your smell.

You are a dainty *Violet*,
Yet wither'd, ere you can be set
Within the Virgin's Coronet.

You are the *Queen* all flowers among,
But die you must (faire Maid) ere long,
As He, the maker of this Song.

TO BE MERRY.

*L*ETS now take our time ;
    While w'are in our Prime ;
And old, old Age is a farre off :
    For the evill evill dayes
    Will come on apace ;
Before we can be aware of.

*G*ET up, get up for shame, the Blooming Morne
Upon her wings presents the god unshorne.
See how *Aurora* throwes her faire
Fresh-quilted colours through the aire :
Get up, sweet-Slug-a-bed, and see
The Dew-bespangling Herbe and Tree.
Each Flower has wept, and bow'd toward the East,
Above an houre since ; yet you not drest,
Nay ! not so much as out of bed ?
When all the Birds have Mattens seyd,
And sung their thankfull Hymnes : 'tis sin,

Nay,

5   69

Nay, profanation to keep in,
When as a thousand Virgins on this day,
Spring, sooner than the Lark, to fetch in May.

Rise ;

Rise ; and put on your Foliage, and be seene
To come forth, like the Spring-time, fresh and greene ;
    And sweet as *Flora*.   Take no care
    For Jewels for your Gowne, or Haire :
    Feare not ; the leaves will strew
    Gemms in abundance upon you :
Besides, the childhood of the Day has kept,
Against you come, some *Orient Pearls* unwept :
    Come, and receive them while the light
    Hangs on the Dew-locks of the night :
    And *Titan* on the Eastern hill
    Retires himselfe, or else stands still
Till you come forth.   Wash, dresse, be briefe in praying :
Few Beads are best, when once we goe a Maying.

Come,

Come, my *Corinna*, come ; and coming, marke
How each field turns a street ; each street a Parke
    Made green, and trimm'd with trees : see how
    Devotion gives each House a Bough,
    Or Branch : Each Porch, each doore, ere this
    An Arke a Tabernacle is
Made up of white-thorn neatly enterwove ;
As if here were those cooler shades of love.
    Can such delights be in the street,
    And open fields, and we not see't ?
    Come, we'll abroad ; and let's obay
    The Proclamation made for May :
And sin no more, as we have done, by staying ;
But my *Corinna*, come, let's goe a Maying.

                                  There's

There's not a budding Boy, or Girle, this day,
But is got up, and gone to bring in May.
  A deale of Youth, ere this, is come
  Back, with *White-thorn* laden home.
  Some have dispatcht their Cakes and Creame,
  Before that we have left to dreame :
And some have wept, and woo'd, and plighted Troth,
And chose their Priest, ere we can cast off sloth ·
  Many a green-gown has been given ;
  Many a kisse, both odde and even :
  Many a glance too has been sent
  From out the eye, Loves Firmament :
Many a jest told of the Keyes betraying
This night, and Locks pickt, yet w'are not a Maying.

L A Abby

Come,

Come, let us goe, while we are in our prime ;
And take the harmlesse follie of the time.
    We shall grow old apace, and die
    Before we know our liberty.
    Our life is short ; and our dayes run
    As fast away as do's the Sunne :
And as a vapour, or a drop of raine
Once lost, can ne'r be found againe :
    So when or you or I are made
    A fable, song, or fleeting shade ;
    All love, all liking, all delight
    Lies drown'd with us in endlesse night.
Then while time serves, and we are but decaying ;
Come, my *Corinna*, come, let's goe a Maying.

GOOD morrow to the Day so fair ;
   Good morning Sir to you :
   Good morrow to mine own torn hair
   Bedabled with the dew.

Good morning to this Prim-rose too ;
   Good morrow to each maid ;
That will with flowers the *Tomb* bestrew,
   Wherein my Love is laid.

Ah woe is me, woe, woe is me,
   Alack and welladay !
For pitty, Sir, find out that Bee,
   Which bore my Love away.

I'le seek him in your *Bonnet* brave ;
   Ile seek him in your eyes ;
Nay, now I think th'ave made his grave
   I'th'bed of strawburies.

Ile seek him there ; I know, ere this,
      The cold, cold Earth doth shake him ;
But I will go, or send a kisse
   By you, Sir, to awake him.

Pray hurt him not ; though he be dead,
   He knowes well who do love him,
And who with green-turfes reare his head,
   And who do rudely move him.

He's soft and tender (Pray take heed)
   With bands of Cow-slips bind him ;
And bring him home, but 'tis decreed,
   That I shall never find him.

THE SAD MAYDES SONGE

Guode morrow to the day so faire,
Good morrow Sir to you,
Good morrow to mine owne torne haire,
All dabbled in the deaw.

Good morrow to this cowslip too,
Good morrow to each maide
That will with teares the tombe bestrew
Wherein my love was layed.

Ah woe is me, woe, woe is me,
Alacke and well a day,
For pitty, sir, finde out that bee
Which bore my love away.

Ile seeke him in your bonnet brave,
Ile seeke him in your eyes,
Nay, now I thinke th'have made his grave
I'th bedd of strawberries.

Ile seeke him there, I hope ere this
The cold cold earth doth take him,
But I will goe, or send a kisse,
By you, sir, to awake him.

Pray hurt him not, though he be dead,
He knowes well who doth love him,
And who with greene turffes reares
his head,
And who doth rudely move him.

Hee's soft and tender, pray take heed,
With bands of balme bind him,
And bringe him home, but tis decreed,
That I shall never finde him.

Roh. Herrick.

A BUCOLICK BETWIXT TWO:

Lacon and Thyrsis.

Lacon. FOR a kiss or two, confesse,
         What doth cause this pensiveness?
         Thou most lovely Neat-heardesse:
Why so lonely on the hill?
Why thy pipe by thee so still,
That ere while was heard so shrill?

Tell me, do thy kine now fail
To fulfill the milkin-paile?
Say, what is't that thou do'st aile?

Thyr. None of these; but out, alas!
A mischance is come to pass,
And I'le tell thee what it was:
See mine eyes are weeping ripe,
Lacon. Tell, and I'le lay down my Pipe.

Thyr. I have lost my lovely steere,
That to me was far more deer
Then these kine, which I milke here.
Board of fore-head, large of eye,
Party colour'd like a Pie;
Smooth in each limb as a die;
Clear of hoof, and clear of horn;
Sharply pointed as a thorn:
With a neck by yoke unworn.
From the which hung down by strings,
Balls of Cowslips, Daisie rings,
Enterplac't with ribbanings.
Faultless every way for shape;
Not a straw co'd him escape;
Ever gamesome as an ape:

But

83

But yet harmless as a sheep,
(Pardon, *Lacon* if I weep)
Tears will spring, where woes are deep.
Now (ai me) (ai me.) Last night
Came a mad dog, and did bite,
I, and kil'd my dear delight.

Lacon. Alack for grief !
Thyr. But I'le be brief,

Hence I must, for time doth call
Me, and my sad Play-mates all,
To his Ev'ning Funerall.
Live long, *Lacon*, so *adew.*
Lacon. Mournful maid farewell to you ;
Earth afford ye flowers to strew.

THE *PARCÆ, or, THREE DAINTY DESTINIES:*
THE *ARMILET.*

*T*HREE lovely Sisters working were
    (As they were closely set)
Of soft and dainty Maiden-haire,
    A curious *Armelet.*
I smiling, ask'd them what they did ?
    (Faire *Destinies* all three)
Who told me, they had drawn a thred
    of Life, and 'twas for me.
They shew'd me then, how fine 'twas spun ;
    And I reply'd thereto,
I care not now how soone 'tis done,
    Or cut, if cut by you.

Three lovely Sisters workinge were
(As they were closely set)
Of soft and dainty Maiden-haire
A curious Armelet.
I smilinge ask'd them what they did
(Fair Destinies all three) ?
Who told me they had drawn a thread
Of Life, and 'twas for me.
They show'd me then how fine 'twas spun;
And I reply'd there-to
I care not now how soone 'tis done,
Or ever, if ever by yov.

Rob: Herrick

THE WILLOW GARLAND.

A Willow Garland thou did'st send
        Perfum'd (last day) to me :
    Which did but only this portend,
        I was forsooke by thee.

Since so it is ; Ile tell thee what,
        To morrow thou shalt see
Me weare the Willow ; after that,
        To dye upon the Tree.

As Beasts unto the Altars go
        With Garlands drest, so I
Will, with my Willow-wreath also,
        Come forth and sweetly dye.

UPON MRS. ELIZ: WHEELER, UNDER THE
NAME OF AMARILLIS.

S WEET *Amarillis*, by a Spring's
        Soft and soule-melting murmurings,
        Slept ; and thus sleeping, thither flew
A *Robin-Red brest ;* who at view,
Not seeing her at all to stir,
Brought leaves and mosse to cover her :
But while he, perking, there did prie
About the Arch of either eye ;
The lid began to let out day ;
At which poore *Robin* flew amay :
And seeing her not dead, but all disleav'd ;
He chirpt for joy, to see himself disceav'd.

87

A DIALOGUE BETWIXT HIMSELFE AND MISTRESSE ELIZA: WHEELER, UNDER THE NAME OF AMARILLIS

*M*Y dearest Love, since thou wilt go,
  And leave me here behind thee ;
For love or pitie let me know
  The place where I may find thee.

Amaril. In country Meadowes pearl'd with Dew,
  And set about with Lillies ;
There filling Maunds with Cowslips, you
  May find your *Amarillis.*

Her. What have the Meades to do with thee,
  Or with thy youthfull houres ?
Live thou at Court, where thou mayst be
  The *Queen* of men, not flowers.

Let Country wenches make'em fine
  With Posies, since 'tis fitter
For thee with richest Jemmes to shine,
  And like the Starres to glitter.

Amaril. You set too high a rate upon
  A Shepheardess so homely ;
Her. Believe it (dearest) ther's not one
  I'th' Court that's halfe so comly.

I prithee stay. *(Am.)* I must away,
  Lets kiss first, then we'l sever.
Ambo. And though we bid adieu to day,
  Wee shall not part for ever.

88

Rob: Herrick ——— I ———
A DIALOGVE · BETWIXT · HIMSELFE · & · MISTRESSE · ELIZA · WHEELER · VNDER
Ye · NAME · OF · AMARILLIS

My dearest loue, since thou wilt go,
And leaue me heare behind thee;
For loue or pitie let me know
   The place where I may find thee

AMARIL

In country meadowes pearl'd with dew,
And set about with lillies; for
There filling mavnds with cow-slips,
You may find your Amarillis.

HER:

What haue the meades to do with thee,
Or with thy youthfull howres? liue
Liue thou at Court where thou mayst
   The qveen of menne, not flowers.

Let country wenches make 'em fine
   With poesies since 'tis fitter
For thee with richest jemmes to shine
   And like ye hauen to glitter.

AMARIL:

You set too high a Rate vpon
   A shepheardesse so homely

HER

Beleiue it, dearest, there's not one
   I'th' Court that's halfe so comly

I prithee stay AMARIL: I must away
   Let's Kisse first then we'l seuer

AMBO

And tho' we bid adiu today
   Wee shall not part foreuer

E. A. ABBEY SEP: 12: 1880

*T*HESE fresh beauties (we can prove)
   Once were Virgins sick of love,
   Turn'd to Flowers. Still in some
Colours goe, and colours come.

I CALL AND I CALL.

I Call, I call, who doe ye call?
   The Maids to catch this Cowslip-ball:
   But since these Cowslips fading be,
Troth, leave the flowers, and Maids, take me.
Yet, if that neither you will doe,
Speak but the word, and Ile take you.

THE OLD WIVES PRAYER.

*H*OLY-ROOD come forth and shield
    Us i'th'Citie, and the Field :
    Safely guard us, now and aye,
From the blast that burns by day ;
And those sounds that us affright.
In the dead of dampish night
Drive all hurtfull Feinds us fro,
By the Time the Cocks first crow.

CEREMONY UPON CANDLEMAS EVE.

*D*OWN with the Rosemary, and so
    Down with the Baies, & mistletoe :
    Down with the Holly, Ivie, all,
Wherewith ye drest the Christmas Hall :
That so the superstitious find
No one least Branch there left behind :
For look how many leaves there be
Neglected there (maids trust to me)
So many *Goblins* you shall see.

CHRISTMAS-EVE, ANOTHER CEREMONIE.

*C*OME guard this night the Christmas-Pie,
    That the Thiefe, though ne'r so slie,
    With his Flesh-hooks, don't come nie
                    To catch it

From him, who all alone sits there,
Having his eyes still in his eare,
And a deale of nightly feare
                    To watch it.

DECAN-BOURN, A RUDE RIVER IN DEVON. BY WHICH SOMETIMES HE LIVED.

*D*ECAN-BOURN, farewell ; I never look to see
    Deane, or thy warty incivility.
    Thy rockie bottome, that doth teare thy streams,
And makes them frantick, ev'n to all extreames ;
To my content, I never sho'd behold,
Were thy streames silver, or thy rocks all gold.
Rockie thou art ; and rockie we discover
Thy men ; and rockie are thy wayes all over.
O men, O manners ; Now, and ever knowne
To be *A Rockie Generation !*
A people currish ; churlish as the seas ;
And rude (almost) as rudest Salvages.
With whom I did, and may re-sojourne when
Rockes turn to Rivers, Rivers turn to Men.

TO HIS MAID PREW.

*T*HESE *Summer-Birds* did with thy Master stay
  The times of warmth ; but then they flew away ;
  Leaving their Poet (being now grown old)
Expos'd to all the comming Winters cold.
But thou *kind Prew* did'st with my Fates abide,
As well the Winters, as the Summers Tide :
For which thy Love, live with thy Master here,
Not two, but all the seasons of the yeare.

UPON PRUDENCE BALDWIN.

HER SICKNESSE.

*P*RUE, my dearest Maid, is sick,
  Almost to a Lunatick :
  Æsculapius ! come and bring
Means for her recovering ;
And a gallant Cock shall be
Offer'd up by Her, to Thee.

UPON PREW HIS MAID.

*I*N this little Urne is laid
  Prewdence Baldwin (once my maid)
  From whose happy spark here let
Spring the purple Violet.

To His Mayde Prew

These svmmer-birds did with thy master stay
The times of warmth; but then they flew away;
Leauing their poet being now grown old
Expos'd to all the comming winters cold
But thou, kind Prew, did'n with my fates abide
As well the winters as the svmmers tide
For which thy loue, liue with thy master here
Not two but all the seafons of the yeare

R. Herrick

TO PRIMROSES FILL'D WITH MORNING DEW.

WHY doe ye weep, sweet Babes? can Tears
      Speak griefe in you,
    Who were but borne
  Just as the modest Morne
  Teem'd her refreshing dew?
Alas you have not known that shower,
      That marres a flower;
    Nor felt th'unkind
  Breath of a blasting wind;
  Nor are ye worne with yeares;
      Or warpt, as we,
    Who think it strange to see,
Such pretty flowers, (like to Orphans young)
To speak by Teares, before ye have a Tongue.

  Speak, whimp'ring Younglings, and make known
      The reason, why
    Ye droop, and weep;
  Is it for want of sleep?
  Or childish Lullabie;
  Or that ye have not seen as yet
      The *Violet?*
    Or brought a kisse
  From that Sweet-heart, to this?
  No, no, this sorrow shown
      By your teares shed,
    Wo'd have this Lecture read,
That things of greatest, so of meanest worth,
Conceiv'd with grief are, and with teares brought forth.

TO VIOLETS.

WELCOME Maids of Honour,
    You doe bring
    In the Spring ;
And wait upon her.

She has Virgins many,
    Fresh and faire ;
    Yet you are
More sweet then any.

Y'are the Maiden Posies,
    And so grac't,
    To be plac't,
'Fore Damask Roses.

Yet though thus respected,
    By and by
    Ye doe lie,
Poore Girles, neglected.

UPON LOVE.

I HELD Love's head while it did ake ;
    But so it chanc't to be ;
The cruell paine did his forsake,
And forthwith came to me.

Ai me ! How shal my griefe be stil'd ?
    Or where else shall we find
One like to me, who must be kill'd
    For being too—too—kind ?

102

THE PRIMROSE.

ASKE me why I send you here
This sweet *Infanta* of the yeere ?
Aske me why I send to you
This Primrose, thus bepearl'd with dew ?
I will whisper to your eares,
The sweets of Love are mixt with tears.

Ask me why this flower do's show
So yellow-green, and sickly too ?
Ask me why the stalk is weak
And bending, (yet it doth not break ?
I will answer, These discover
What fainting hopes are in a Lover.

TO MISTRESSE KATHERINE BRADSHAW,
THE LOVELY, THAT CROWNED
HIM WITH LAUREL.

MY Muse in Meads has spent her many houres,
Sitting, and sorting severall sorts of flowers,
To make for others garlands ; and to set
On many a head here, many a Coronet :
But, amongst All encircled here, not one
Gave her a day of Coronation ;
Till you (sweet Mistresse) came and enterwove
A *Laurel* for her, (ever young as love)
You first of all crown'd her ; she must of due,
Render for that, a crowne of life to you.

A VOW TO VENUS.

*H*APPILY I had a sight
Of my dearest deare last night;
Make her this day smile on me,
And Ile Roses give to thee.

UPON MISTRESSE SUSANNA SOUTHWELL HER CHEEKS.

*R*ARE are thy cheeks *Susanna*, which do show
Ripe Cherries smiling, while that others blow.

UPON HER EYES.

*C*LEERE are her eyes,
Like purest Skies.
Discovering from thence
A Babie there
That turns each Sphere,
Like an Intelligence.

UPON HER FEET.

*H*ER pretty feet
Like snailes did creep
A little out, and then,
As if they played at Bo-peep,
Did soon draw in agen.

Vpon·Mistresse·Susanna·Southwell·her·Cheeks·

Rare are thy Cheeks Susanna which do shew
Ripe Cherries smiling while that others blow

·Vpon·her·Eies·

Cleere are her eies
  Like purest skies
Discouering from thence
  A babie there
  That turns each sphere
Like an intelligence

·Vpon·her·Feet·

Her pretty feet
  Like snailes did creep
  A little out, and then
As if they played at bo-peep
Did soon draw in agen

HOW PRIMROSES CAME GREEN.

*V*IRGINS, time-past, known were these,
  Troubled with Green-sicknesses,
 ' Turn'd to flowers : Stil the hieu,
  Sickly Girles, they beare of you.

A CANTICLE TO APOLLO.

PLAY Phœbus on thy Lute ;
  And we will, all sit mute :
  By listning to thy Lire,
  That sets all eares on fire.

Hark, harke, the God do's play !
And as he leads the way
Through heaven, the very Spheres,
As men, turne all to eares.

UPON JULIA'S VOICE.

SO smooth, so sweet, so silv'ry is thy voice,
  As, could they hear, the Damn'd would make no noise,
  But listen to thee, (walking in thy chamber)
  Melting melodious words, to Lutes of Amber.

ANOTHER UPON HER WEEPING.

SHE by the River sate, and sitting there,
  She wept, and made it deeper by a teare.

She by the River sate & sitting there
She Wept & made it deeper by a Teare

TO ELECTRA.

I dare not ask a kisse ;
  I dare not beg a smile ;
  Lest having that, or this,
  I might grow proud the while.

No, no, the utmost share
  Of my desire, shall be
Onely to kisse that Aire,
  That lately kissed thee.

ON LOVE.

L OVE bade me aske a gift,
  And I no more did move,
  But this, that I might shift
  Still with my clothes, my Love :
That favour granted was ;
  Since which, though I love many,
Yet so it comes to passe,
  That long I love not any.

UPON HIMSELF.

T HOU shalt not All die ; for while Love's fire shines
  Upon his Altar, men shall read thy lines ;
  And learn'd Musicians shall to honour *Herricks*
  Fame, and his Name, both set and sing his Lyricks.

113

THE RAINBOW: OR CURIOUS COVENANT.

*M*INE eyes, like clouds, were drizling raine
    And as they thus did entertaine
    The gentle Beams from *Julia's* sight
To mine eyes level'd opposite :
O Thing admir'd ! there did appeare
A curious Rainbow smiling there ;
Which was the Covenant, that she
No more wo'd drown mine eyes, or me.

THE BRACELET TO JULIA.

*W*HY I tye about thy wrist,
    Julia, this my silken twist
    For what other reason is't,
But to shew thee how in part,
Thou my pretty Captive art?
But thy Bondslave is my heart :
'Tis but silke that bindeth thee,
Knap the thread, and thou art free :
But 'tis otherwise with me ;
I am bound, and fast bound so,
That from thee I cannot go ;
If I co'd, I wo'd not so.

THE ROSARIE.

*O*NE ask'd me where the Roses grew ?
    I bade him not goe seek ;
    But forthwith bade my *Julia* shew
    A bud in either cheek.

When I tye about thy wrift,
Ivlia, this my filken twift;
For what other reafon is't
Bvt to fhew thee how in part,
Thou my prettie captyue art?
Bvt thy bondflaue is my hearte:
'Tis bvt filke that bindeth thee,
Knap the thread, and thov art free:
Bvt 'tis otherwife with me;
I am bovnd, and faft hevnd fo
That from thee I cannot goe,
If I cod, I wod not fo.

R. Herrick

*Y*OU may vow Ile not forgett
            To pay the debt,
        Which to thy Memorie stands as due
            As faith can seale It you
Take then tribute of my teares
            So long as I have feares
            To prompt mee, I shall euer
Languish and looke but thy returne see neuer
            Oh then to lessen my dispaire
            Print thy lips Into the ayre
                    So by this
Meanes I may kisse thy kisse
            when as some kinde
                    winde
Shall hither waft it and In liew
My lipps shall send a 1000 back to you.

                            Ro : herrick.

HIS REQUEST TO JULIA

*I*VLIA, if I chance to die
        Ere I print my Poetry ;
        I most humbly thee desire
To commit it to the fire :
Better 'twere my Book were dead,
Then to live not perfected.

UPON HIS KINSWOMAN MISTRIS ELIZABETH HERRICK.

SWEET virgin, that I do not set
    The pillars up of weeping *Jet*,
    Or mournfull *Marble;* let thy shade
Not wrathfull seem, or fright the Maide,
Who hither at her wonted howers
Shall come to strew thy earth with flowers.
No, know (Blest Maide) when there's not one
Remainder left of Brasse or stone,
Thy living Epitaph shall be,
Though lost in them, yet found in me.
Dear, in thy *bed of Roses*, then,
Till this world shall dissolve as men,
Sleep, while we hide thee from the light,
Drawing thy curtains round : *Good night.*

ANTHEA'S RETRACTION.

ANTHEA laught, and fearing lest excesse
    Might stretch the cords of civill comelinesse:
    She with a dainty blush rebuk't her face ;
    And cal'd each line back to his *rule* and *space.*

TO ANTHEA.

SICK is *Anthea*, sickly is the spring, :
    The Primrose sick, and sickly every thing :
    The while my deer *Anthea* do's but droop,
The *Tulips, Lillies, Daffadills* do *stoop ;*
But when again sh'as got her healthfull houre,
Each bending then, will rise a proper flower.

Sick is Anthea sickly is the Spring
The primrose sick, & sickly every thing
The while my dear Anthea do's but droop
The tulips lillies daffodills do stoop;
But when again sh'as got her healthfull howre
Each bending then, will rise a proper flower

THE WAKE.

COME *Anthea* let us two
Go to Feast, as others do.
Tarts and Custards, Creams and Cakes,
Are the Junketts still at Wakes :
Unto which the Tribes resort,
Where the businesse is the sport :
Morris-dancers thou shalt see,
Marian too in Pagentrie :
And a Mimick to devise
Many grinning properties.
Players there will be, and those
Base in action as in clothes :
Yet with strutting they will please
The incurious Villages.
Neer the dying of the day,
There will be a *Cudgell*-Play,
Where a *Coxcomb* will be broke,
Ere a good *word* can be spoke :
But the anger ends all here,
Drencht in Ale, or drown'd in Beere.
Happy Rusticks, best content
With the cheapest Merriment :
And possesse no other feare,
Then to want the Wake next Yeare.

UPON MUCH-MORE. EPIG.

MUCH-MORE, provides, and hoords up like an Ant;
Yet *Much-more* still complains he is in want.
Let *Much-more* justly pay his tythes; then try
How both his Meale and Oile will multiply.

TO JULIA.

PERMIT me, *Julia*, now to goe away ;
    Or by thy love, decree me here to stay.
    If thou wilt say, that I shall live with thee ;
Here shall my endless Tabernacle be :
If not, (as banisht) I will live alone
There, where no language ever yet was known.

THE NIGHT-PIECE, TO JULIA.

HER Eyes the Glow-worme lend thee,
    The Shooting Starres attend thee ;
        And the Elves also,
        Whose little eyes glow,
Like the sparks of fire, befriend thee.

    No *Will-o'th'- Wispe* mis-light thee ;
    Nor Snake, or Slow-worme bite thee :
        But on, on thy way
        Not making a stay,
Since Ghost ther's none to affright thee.

    Let not the darke thee cumber ;
    What though the Moon do's slumber ?
        The Starres of the night
        Will lend thee their light,
Like Tapers cleare without number.

    Then *Julia* let me wooe thee,
    Thus, thus to come unto me :
        And when I shall meet
        Thy silv'ry feet,
My soule Ile poure into thee.

E·A·Abbey

The Night-piece to Julia

Her eyes the glow-worm lend thee
   The shooting starres attend thee
      And the Elves also
      Whose little eyes glow
Like the sparkes of fire befriend thee

        No Will o' th' Wispe mis-light thee
        Nor Snake or Slow-worm bite thee
           But on, on thy way
           Not making a stay
        Since Ghost there's none to affright thee

              Let not the darke thee cumber
              What though the Moon do's slumber
                 The starres of the night
                 Will lend thee their light
              Like tapers cleare without number

                    Then Julia let me wooe thee
                    Thus, thus to come unto thee
                       And when I shall meet
                       Thy silu'ry feet,
                    My soule I'le povre into thee

I Have lost, and lately, these
    Many dainty Mistresses :
    Stately *Julia*, prime of all ;
Sapho next, a principall :
Smooth *Anthea*, for a skin
White, and Heaven-like Chrystalline :
Sweet *Electra*, and the choice
Myrha, for the Lute, and Voice.
Next, *Corinna*, for her wit,
And the graceful use of it :
With *Perilla :* All are gone :
Onely *Herrick's* left alone,
For to number sorrow by
Their departures hence, and die.

TO THE REVEREND SHADE OF HIS
RELIGIOUS FATHER.

T HAT for seven *Lusters* I did never come
    To doe the *Rites* to thy Religious Tombe :
    That neither haire was cut, or true teares shed
By me, o'r thee, *(as justments to the dead)*
Forgive, forgive me ; since I did not know
Whether thy bones had here their Rest, or no.
But now 'tis known, Behold ; behold, I bring
Unto thy Ghost, th'Effused Offering :
And look, what Smallage, Night-shade, Cypresse, Yew,
Unto the shades have been, or now are due,
Here I devote ; And something more then so ;

I

9   125

I come to pay a Debt of Birth I owe.
Thou gav'st me life, (but Mortall ;) For that one
Favour, Ile make a full satisfaction ;
For my life mortall, Rise from out thy Herse,
And take a life immortall from my Verse.

TO LAURELS.

A Funerall stone,
Or Verse I covet none ;
But onely crave
Of you that I may have
A sacred Laurel springing from my grave :
Which being seen,
Blest with perpetuall greene,
May grow to be
Not so much call'd a tree,
As the eternall monument of me.

TO THE LARK.

*G*OOD speed, for I this day
Betimes my Mattens say :
Because I doe
Begin to wooe :
Sweet singing Lark,
Be thou the Clark,
And know thy when
To say, *Amen*.
And if I prove
Blest in my love ;
Then thou shalt be
High-Priest to me,
At my returne,
To Incense burne ;
And so to solemnize
Love's, and my Sacrifice.

THE FAIRIES.

*I*F ye will with *Mab* find grace,
Set each Platter in his place :
Rake the Fier up, and get
Water in, ere Sun be set.
Wash your Pailes, and clense your Dairies ;
Sluts are loathsome to the Fairies :
Sweep your house : Who doth not so,
Mab will pinch her by the toe.

127

CHARMS.

BRING the holy crust of Bread,
Lay it underneath the head ;
'Tis a certain charm to keep ·
Hags away, while Children sleep.

ANOTHER CEREMONIE.

WASSAILE the Trees, that they may beare
You many a Plum, and many a Peare :
For more or lesse fruits they will bring,
As you doe give them Wassailing.

UPON PEASON. EPIG.

LONG Locks of late our Zelot *Peason* weares,
Not for to hide his high and mighty eares ;
No, but because he wo'd not have it seen,
That Stubble stands, where once large eares have been.

UPON AN OLD WOMAN.

OLD widdow *Prouse* to do her neighbours evill
Wo'd give (some say) her soule unto the Devill.
Well, when sh'as kild, that Pig, Goose, Cock or Hen,
What wo'd she give to get that soule agen ?

TO AN OLD WOMAN

Old Widdow Provse to do her neighbors
    euill
Ha'd giue some say her soul vnto ỹ
    deuill
Well when sh'as kil'd that pigge
    goose cocke or hen
What wo'd she giue to get that fovle
    againe

Rob: Hearicke.

*N*OW, now the mirth comes
    With the cake full of plums,
Where Beane's the *King* of the sport here ;
    Beside we must know,
    The Pea also
Must revell, as *Queene*, in the Court here.

    Begin then to chuse,
    (This night as ye use)
Who shall for the present delight here,
    Be a *King* by the lot,
    And who shall not
Be Twelfe-day *Queene* for the night here.

    Which knowne, let us make,
    Joy-sops with the cake ;
And let not a man then be seen here,
    Who unurg'd will not drinke
    To the base from the brink
A health to the King and the Queene here.

    Next crowne the bowle full
    With gentle lambs-wooll ;
Adde sugar, nutmeg and ginger,
    With store of ale too ;
    And thus ye must doe
To make the wassaile a swinger.

    Give then to the King
    And Queene wassailing ;
And though with ale ye be whet here ;
    Yet part ye from hence,
    As free from offence,
As when ye innocent met here.

CONTENT, NOT CATES.

'TIS not the food, but the content
That makes the Tables merriment.
Where Trouble serves the board, we eate
The Platters there, as soone as meat.
A little Pipkin with a bit
Of Mutton, or of Veale in it,
Set on my Table, (Trouble-free)
More then a Feast contenteth me.

JACK AND JILL.

SINCE Jack and Jill both wicked be ;
It seems a wonder unto me,
That they no better do agree.

HIS COMFORT.

THE only comfort of my life
Is that I never yet had wife ;
Nor will hereafter ; since I know
Who Weds, ore-buyes his weal with woe.

UPON TAP.

TAP (better known than trusted) as we heare
Sold his old Mothers Spectacles for Beere :
And not unlikely ; rather too then fail,
He'l sell her Eyes, and Nose, for Beere and Ale.

Vpon Tap

Tap (better known than trvsted) as we heare,
Sold his old Mother's spectacles for beere:
And not vnlikely; rather too than fail,
He'l sell her Eyes and Nose for Beer and Ale.

TO ANTHEA.

ANTHEA I am going hence
With some small stock of innocence:
But yet those blessed gates I see
Withstanding entrance unto me.
To pray for me doe thou begin,
The Porter then will let me in.

HIS WISH TO PRIVACIE.

GIVE me a Cell
        To dwell,
Where no foot hath
        A path :
There will I spend,
        And end
My wearied yeares
        In teares.

135

SPUR jingles now, and sweares by no meane oathes,
　　He's double honour'd, since h'as got gay cloathes :
　　Most like his Suite, and all commend the Trim ;
And thus they praise the Sumpter ; but not him :
As to the Goddesse, people did conferre
Worship, and not to'th' Asse that carried her.

TO HIS BOOKE.

T'AKE mine advise, and go not neere
　　Those faces (sower as Vineger.)
　　For these, and Nobler numbers can
　　Ne'r please the *supercillious* man.

TO MY ILL READER.

THOU say'st my lines are hard ;
　　And I the truth will tell ;
　　They are both hard, and marr'd,
　　If thou not read'st them well.

· Vpon Spvr ·

Spvr jingles nowe, and sweares by no mean oaths
He's double-honovr'd, since h'as got Gay Cloathes
Most like hys svite, and all commend the trim
And thvs they praise the svmpter; but not him
As to the Goddesse people did conferre
Worship, and not to'th' asse that carried her

TO DIANEME.

SWEET, be not proud of those two eyes,
Which Star-like sparkle in their skies :
Nor be you proud, that you can see
All hearts your captives ; yours, yet free :
Be you not proud of that rich haire,
Which wantons with the Love-sick aire :
When as that *Rubie*, which you weare,
Sunk from the tip of your soft eare,
Will last to be a precious Stone,
When all your world of Beautie's gone.

UPON CUFFE. EPIG.

*C*UFFE comes to Church much ; but he keeps his bed
Those Sundayes onely, when as Briefs are read.
This makes *Cuffe* dull ; and troubles him the most,
Because he cannot sleep i'th'Church, free-cost.

UPON THE DETRACTER.

I ask't thee oft, what Poets thou hast read,
And lik'st the best ? Still thou reply'st, The dead.
I shall, ere long, with green turfs cover'd be ;
Then sure thou't like, or thou wilt envie me.

TO A FRIEND.

*L*OOKE in my Book, and herein see,
Life endlesse sign'd to thee and me.
We o're the tombes, and Fates shall flye ;
While other generations dye.

Vpon Cvffe

Cvffe comes to Chvrch mvch; but
	he keeps his bed
Those Svndays onely, when as
	briefs are read.
This makes Cvffe dull; and
	troubles him the most
Becavse he cannot sleep i'th' Chvrch,
	free-cost.

UPON A MAIDE.

*H*ERE she lyes (in Bed of Spice)
Faire as *Eve* in Paradice :
For her beauty it was such
Poets co'd not praise too much.
Virgins Come, and in a Ring
Her supreamest *Requiem* sing ;
Then depart, but see ye tread
Lightly, lightly ore the dead.

AN EPITAPH UPON A VIRGIN.

*H*ERE a solemne *Fast* we keepe,
While all beauty lyes asleep
Husht be all things ; (no noyse here)
But the toning of a teare :
Or a sigh of such as bring
Cowslips for her covering.

TO HIS GIRLES WHO WOULD HAVE HIM SPORTFULL.

*A*LCAS I can't, for tell me how
  Can I be gamesome (aged now)
  Besides ye see me daily grow
Here Winter-like, to Frost and Snow.
And I ere long, my Girles shall see,
Ye quake for cold to looke on me.

LYRICK FOR LEGACIES.

*G*OLD I've none, for use or show,
  Neither Silver to bestow
  At my death ; but thus much know,
That each Lyrick here shall be
Of my love a Legacie,
Left to all posterity.
Gentle friends, then doe but please,
To accept such coynes as these ;
As my last Remembrances.

To his Girles who would haue him sportfvll

Alas! I can't, for tell me how
Can I be gamesome, aged now;
Besides, ye see me daily grow
Here, winter-like, to frost and snow
And I ere long, my girles, shall see
Ye qvake for cold to looke on me

THE COMMING OF GOOD LUCK.

SO Good-luck came, and on my roofe did light,
Like noyse-lesse Snow ; or as the dew of night :
Not all at once, but gently, as the trees
Are, by the Sun-beams, tickel'd by degrees.

THE POWER IN THE PEOPLE.

LET Kings Command, and doe the best they may,
The saucie Subjects still will beare the sway.

ILL GOVERNMENT.

PREPOSTEROUS is that Government, (and rude)
When Kings obey the wilder Multitude.

LOSSE FROM THE LEAST.

GREAT men by small meanes oft are overthrown :
He's Lord of thy life, who contemnes his own.

TO OENONE.

WHAT Conscience, say, is it in thee
 When I a Heart had one,
To Take away that Heart from me,
 And to retain thy own ?

For shame or pitty now encline
 To play a loving part ;
Either to send me kindly thine,
 Or give me back my heart.

Covet not both ; but if thou dost
 Resolve to part with neither ;
Why ! yet to shew that thou art just,
 Take me and mine together.

THE BRIDE-CCAKE.

THIS day my *Julia* thou must make
 For Mistresse Bride, the wedding Cake :
 Knead but the Dow and it will be
To paste of Almonds turn'd by thee :
Or kisse it thou, but once, or twice,
And for the Bride-Cake ther'l be Spice.

148

The Bride-Cake

This day, my Julia thou must make
For mistresse bride the wedding-cake
Knead but the dow and it will be
To paste of almonds turnd by thee
Or kisse it thou but once or twice
And for the bride-cake ther'l be spice

I Send, I send here my supremest kiss
   To thee my *silver-footed Thamasis*.
      No more shall I reiterate thy Strand,
Whereon so many Stately Structures stand :
Nor in the summers sweeter evenings go,
To bath in thee (as thousand others doe.)
No more shall I a long thy christall glide,
In Barge (with boughes and rushes beautifi'd)
With soft smooth Virgins (for our chast disport)
To *Richmond, Kingstone*, and to *Hampton-Court:*
Never againe shall I with Finnie-Ore
Put from, or draw unto the faithfull shore :
And Landing here, or safely Landing there,
Make my way to my *Beloved Westminster :*
Or to the *Golden-cheap-side*, where the earth
Of *Julia Herrick* gave to me my Birth.
May all clean *Nimphs* and curious water Dames,
With Swan-like-state, flote up & down thy streams:
No drought upon thy wanton waters fall
To make them Leane, and languishing at all.
No ruffling winds come hither to discease
Thy pure, and *Silver-wristed Naides*.
Keep up your state ye streams ; and as ye spring,
Never make sick your Banks by surfeiting.
Grow young with Tydes, and though I see ye never,
Receive this vow, *so fare-ye-well for ever*.

CHERRIE-RIPE.

*C*HERRIE-RIPE, Ripe, Ripe, I cry,
    Full and faire ones ; come and buy :
    If so be, you ask me where
They doe grow ? I answer, There,
Where my *Julia's* lips doe smile ;
There's the Land, or Cherry-Ile :
Whose Plantations fully show
All the yeere, where Cherries grow.

HOW PANSIES OR HEATS-EASE CAME FIRST.

*F*ROLLICK Virgins once these were,
    Over-loving, (living here :)
    Being here their ends deny'd
Ranne for Sweet-hearts mad, and dy'd.
Love in pitie of their teares,
And their losse in blooming yeares ;
For their restlesse here-spent houres,
Gave them *Hearts-ease* turn'd to Flow'rs.

How Heartsease came First.

Frollick Virgins once these were,
Ouer-louing, liuing here;
Being here their ends deny'd
Ranne for sweethearts mad, & dy'd.
Loue in pitie of their teares,
And their losse in blooming yeares,
For their restlesse here-spent-houres
Gaue them Heartsease turn'd to flowers.

Rob: Herrick

TO ROBIN RED-BREST.

L AID out for dead, let thy last kindnesse be
With leaves and mosse-work for to cover me:
And while the Wood-nimphs my cold corps inter,
Sing thou my Dirge, sweet-warbling Chorister !
For Epitaph, in Foliage, next write this,
Here, here the Tomb of Robin Herrick is.

THE SADNESSE OF THINGS FOR SAPHO'S SICKNESSE

L ILLIES will languish ; Violets look ill ;
Sickly the Prim-rose : Pale the Daffadill :
That gallant Tulip will hang down his head,
Like to a Virgin newly ravished.
Pansies will weep ; and Marygolds will wither ;
And keep a Fast, and Funerall together,
If *Sapho* droop ; Daisies will open never,
But bid Good-night, and close their lids for ever.

TO CARNCATIONS. A SONG.

STAY while ye will, or goe ;
　　And leave no scent behind ye :
　　Yet trust me ; I shall know
　　　The place, where I may find ye.

Within my *Lucia's* cheek,
　(Whose Livery ye weare)
Play ye at *Hide* or *Seek*,
　I'm sure to find ye there.

TO SAPHO.

SAPHO, I will chuse to go
　Where the Northern winds do blow
　Endlesse Ice, and endlesse Snow :
Rather then I wonce wo'd see,
But a Winters face in thee,
To bennumme my hopes and me.

ON CHLORIS WALKING IN THE SNOW.

I saw faire *Chloris* walke alone,
　When feather'd raine came softly down,
　Then *Jove* descended from his Tower,
To court her in a silver shower,
The wanton snow flew to her brest,
Like little birds into their nest ;
But overcome with whitenes there,
For greife it thaw'd into a teare,
Then falling down her garment hem,
To deck her, froze into a gem.

156

On Chloris Walkinge in y̆ Snowe

I Saw faire Chloris walke alone
When feather'd raine came softly downe,
Then Ioue defcended from his tower
To covrt Her in a filuer ſhower,
The Wanton ſnowe flew to her breft
Like little birds into their neſt;
Bvt ouercome with whitenes there,
For Griefe it thawed into a Teare,
Then falling down her Garment Hem.
To decke her, froʒe into a gem.

R. Herrick.

HOW ROSES CAME RED.

*R*OSES at first were white,
 Till they co'd not agree,
Whether my *Sapho's* breast,
 Or they more white sho'd be.

But being vanquisht quite,
 A blush their cheeks bespred ;
Since which (beleeve the rest)
 The *Roses* first came red.

HOW VIOLETS CAME BLEW.

*L*OVE on a day (wise Poets tell)
 Some time in wrangling spent,
Whether the Violets sho'd excell,
 Or she, in sweetest scent.

But *Venus* having lost the day,
 Poore Girles, she fell on you ;
And beat ye so, (as some dare say)
 Her blowes did make ye blew.

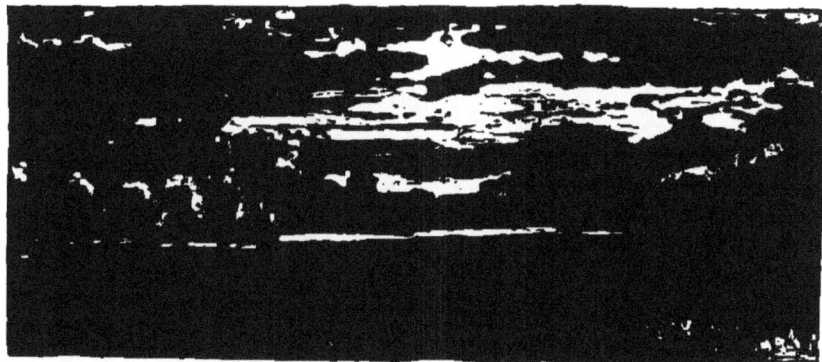

TO PANSIES.

AH! cruell Love ! must I endure
   Thy many scorns, and find no cure ?
   Say, are thy medicines made to be
Helps to all others, but to me ?
Ile leave thee, and to *Pansies* come ;
Comforts you'l afford me some :
You can ease my heart, and doe
What Love co'd ne'r be brought unto.

ON HIMSELFE.

*I*L'E write no more of Love ; but now repent
   Of all those times that I in it have spent.
   Ile write no more of life ; but wish twas ended,
   And that my dust was to the earth commended.

UPON BLANCH.

*B*LANCH swears her Husband's lovely; when a scald
   Has blear'd his eyes : Besides, his head is bald.
   Next, his wilde eares, like Lethern wings full spread,
   Flutter to flie, and beare away his head.

160

Vpon Blanch

Blanch fwears her Hvfbands Iouſy; when
    a ſcald
Has blear'd. his eyes : befides. his head is
    bald
Next, his wilde Eares like Iethern wings
    fvll ſpread
Flvtter to flie and beare away his head

TO SYCCAMORES.

I'M sick of Love ; O let me lie
 Under your shades, to sleep or die !
 Either is welcome ; so I have
Or here my Bed, or here my Grave.
Why do you sigh, and sob, and keep
Time with the tears, that I do weep ?
Say, have ye sence, or do you prove
What *Crucifixions* are in Love ?
I know ye do ; and that's the why,
You sigh for Love, as well as I.

NO LUCK IN LOVE.

I doe love I know not what ;
 Sometimes this, & sometimes that :
 All conditions I aime at.

But, as lucklesse, I have yet
Many shrewd disasters met,
To gaine her whom I wo'd get.

Therefore now Ile love no more,
As I've doted heretofore :
He who must be, shall be poore.

TO CHERRY-BLOSSOMES.

YE may simper, blush, and smile,
 And perfume the aire a while :
 But (sweet things) ye must be gone ;
Fruit, ye know, is comming on :
Then, Ah ! Then, where is your grace,
When as Cherries come in place ?

TO HIS BOOKE.

GOE thou forth my booke, though late ;
    Yet be timely fortunate.
      It may chance good-luck may send
Thee a kinsman, or a friend,
That may harbour thee, when I,
With my fates neglected lye.
If thou know'st not where to dwell,
See, the fier's by : *Farewell.*

TO HIS BOOKE.

MAKE haste away, and let one be
    A friendly Patron unto thee :
      Lest rapt from hence, I see thee lye
Torn for the use of Pasterie ;
Or see thy injur'd Leaves serve well,
To make loose Gownes for Mackarell :
Or see the Grocers in a trice,
Make hoods of thee to serve out Spice.

THE COBLERS CATCH.

COME sit we by the fires side ;
    And roundly drinke we here ;
    Till that we see our cheekes Ale-dy'd
    And noses tann'd with Beere.

The Coblers Catch.

Come Sit we by ye Fires fide
And roundly Drinke wee here;
Till that we fee ovr Cheekes Ale-dy'd,
And Nofes tann'd with Beere.

R Herrick

UPON A CHILD THAT DYED.

*H*ÉRE she lies, a pretty bud,
  Lately made of flesh and blood :
  Who, as soone, fell fast asleep,
As her lirtle *(sic)* eyes did peep.
Give her strewings ; but not stir
The earth, that lightly covers her.

HOW MARIGOLD'S CAME YELLOW.

*I*ÉALOUS *Girles* these sometimes were,
  While they liv'd, or lasted here :
  Turn'd to *Flowers*, still they be
Yellow, markt for Jealousie.

TO MISTRESSE DOROTHY PARSONS.

*I*F thou aske me (Deare) wherefore
  I do write of thee no more :
  I must answer (Sweet) thy part
Lesse is here, then in my heart.

TO HIS NEPHEW TO BE PROSPEROUS IN HIS ART OF PAINTING.

ON, as thou hast begunne, brave youth, and get
The Palme from *Vrbin, Titian, Tintarret,*
Brugel, and *Coxu,* and the workes out-doe,
Of *Holben,* and That mighty *Ruben* too.
So draw, and paint, as none may do the like,
No, not the glory of the World, *Vandike.*

THE DEPARTURE OF THE GOOD DEMON.

WHAT can I do in Poetry,
Now the good Spirit's gone from me ?
Why nothing now, but lonely sit,
And over-read what I have writ.

UPON FONE A SCHOOL-MASTER. EPIG.

FONE sayes, those mighty whiskers he do's weare,
Are twigs of Birch, and willow, growing there :
If so, we'll think too, (when he do's condemne
Boyes to the lash) that he do's whip with them.

Fone sayes those mighty whiskers he do's weare,
Are twigs of birch, and willow, growing there:
Is so, we'll think too, when he do's condemne
Boyes to the lash, that he do's whip with them.

UPON LOVE, BY WAY OF QUESTION AND ANSWER.

I Bring ye love: *Quest.* What will love do?
   Ans. Like, and dislike ye:
   I bring ye love: *Quest.* What will love do?·
   Ans. Stroake ye to strike ye.
I bring ye love: *Quest.* What will love do?
   Ans. Love will be-foole ye:
I bring ye love: *Quest.* What will love do?
   Ans. Heate ye to coole ye:
I bring ye love: *Quest.* What will love do?
   Ans. Love gifts will send ye:
I bring ye love: *Quest.* What will love do?
   Ans. Stock ye to spend ye:
I bring ye love: *Quest.* What will love do?
   Ans. Love will fulfill ye:
I bring ye love: *Quest.* What will love do?
   Ans. Kisse ye, to kill ye.

TO MUSIQUE, TO BECCALME HIS FEVER.

———

C HARME me asleep, and melt me so
   With thy Delicious Numbers;
That being ravisht, hence I goe
Away in easie slumbers.
   Ease my sick head,
   And make my bed,
                                        Thou

Thou Power that canst sever
From me this ill:
And quickly still:
Though thou not kill
My Fever.

Thou sweetly canst convert the same
From a consuming fire,
Into a gentle-licking flame,
And make it thus expire.
Then make me weep
My paines asleep;
And give me such reposes,
That I, poore I,
May think, thereby,
I live and die
'Mongst Roses,

Fall on me like a silent dew,
Or like those Maiden showrs,
Which, by the peepe of day, doe strew
A Baptime o're the flowers.
Melt, melt my paines
With thy soft straines;
That having ease me given,
With full delight,
I leave this light;
And take my flight
For Heaven.

TO MVSIQVE

Noble Numbers.

L OOK how our foule Dayes do exceed our faire ;
And as our bad, more then our good Works are:
Ev'n so those Lines; pen'd by my wanton Wit,
Treble the number of these good I've writ.
Things precious are least num'rous : Men are prone
To do ten Bad, for one Good Action.

A CHRISTMAS CAROLL SUNG TO THE KING IN THE PRESENCE AT WHITE-HALL.

Chor.

W HAT sweeter musick can we bring,
Then a Caroll, for to sing
The Birth of this our heavenly King ?
Awake the Voice ! Awake the String !
Heart, Eare, and Eye, and every thing
Awake ! the while the active Finger
Runs division with the Singer.

From the Flourish they came to the Song.

1   Dark and dull night, flie hence away,
And give the honour to this Day,
That sees *December* turn'd to *May.*

If

175

2   If we may ask the reason, say ;
     The why, and wherefore all things here
     Seem like the Spring-time of the yeere ?

3   Why do's the chilling Winters morne
     Smile, like a field beset with corne ?
     Or smell, like to a Meade new-shorne,
     Thus, on the sudden ?   4. Come and see
     The cause, why things thus fragrant be :
     'Tis He is borne, whose quickning Birth
     Gives life and luster, publike mirth,
     To Heaven, and the under-Earth.

Chor.   We see Him come, and know him ours,
     Who with His Sun-shine and His showers
     Turnes all the patient ground to flowers.

1   The Darling of the world is come,
     And fit it is, we finde a roome
     To welcome Him. The nobler part
     Of all the house here, is the heart,

Chor.   Which we will give Him ; and bequeath
     This Hollie, and this Ivie Wreath,
     To do Him honour ; who's our King,
     Ann Lord of all this Revelling.

         The Musicall Part was composed by
            M. Henry Lawes.

ETERNITIE.

O Yeares ! and Age ! Farewell :
        Behold I go,
        Where I do know
Infinitie to dwell.

                    And

ETERNITIE

Yeares! & Age! farewell:
Behold I goe,
Where I do know
Infinitie to dwell.

And thefe mine Eies fhall fee
All Times, how they
Are loft i'th' Sea
Of vaft Eternitie.

Where neuer Moone fhall
fway
The Starres; but fhe,
And Night, fhall be
Drown'd in one Endleffe Day.

Herrieke

And these mine eyes shall see
　　　All times, how they
　　　Are lost i'th'Sea
Of vast Eternitie.

Where never Moone shall sway
　　　The Starres ; but she,
　　　And Night, shall be
Drown'd in one endlesse Day.

COCK-CROW.

*B*ELL-*MAN* of Night, if I about shall go
　　For to denie my Master, do thou crow.
　　Thou stop'st S. *Peter* in the midst of sin ;
Stay me, by crowing, ere I do begin ;
Better it is, premonish'd, for to shun
A sin, then fall to weeping when 'tis done.

THE BED-MAN, OR GRAVE-MAKER.

*T*HOU hast made many Houses for the Dead ;
　　When my Lot calls me to be buried,
　　For Love or Pittie, prethee let there be
I'th' Church-yard; made, one Tenement for me.

TEMPTATION.

*T*HOSE Saints, which God loves best,
　　The Devill tempts not least.

THE ROSE.

*B*EFORE Mans fall, the Rose was born
(S. *Ambrose* sayes) without the Thorn :
But, for Mans fault, then was the Thorn,
Without the fragrant Rose-bud, born ;
But ne're the Rose without the Thorn.

AN ODE OF THE BIRTH OF OUR SAVIOUR.

*I*N Numbers, and but these few,
I sing Thy Birth, Oh JESU !
Thou prettie Babie, borne here,
With sup'rabundant scorn here :
Who for Thy Princely Port here,
Hadst for Thy place
Of Birth, a base
Out-stable for thy Court here.

Instead of neat Inclosures
Of inter-woven Osiers ;
Instead of fragrant Posies
Of Daffadills, and Roses;
Thy cradle, Kingly Stranger,
As Gospell tells,
Was nothing els.
But, here, a homely manger.

But

But we with Silks, (not Cruells)
With sundry precious Jewells,
And Lilly-work will dresse Thee ;
And as we dispossesse thee
Of clouts, wee'l make a chamber,
            Sweet Babe, for Thee,
            Of Ivorie,
And plaister'd round with Amber.

The Jewes they did disdaine Thee,
But we will entertaine Thee
With Glories to await here
Upon Thy Princely State here,
And more for love, then pittie.
            From yeere to yeere
            Wee'l make Thee, here,
A Free-born of our Citie.

A GRACE FOR A CHILD.

*H*ERE a little child I stand,
    Heaving up my either hand ;
    Cold as paddocks though they be,
Here I lift them up to Thee,
For a benizon to fall
On our meat, and on us all. Amen.

UPON TEARES.

*T*EARES, though th'are here below the sinners brine,
   Above they are the Angels spiced wine.

THE BELL-MAN.

*A*LONG the dark, and silent night,
　　With my Lantern, and my Light,
　　And the trinkling of my Bell,
Thus I walk, and this I tell :
Death and dreadfulnesse call on,
To the gen'rall Session ;
To whose dismall Barre, we there
All accompts must come to cleere :
Scores of sins w'ave made here many,
Wip't out few, (God knowes) if any.
Rise ye Debters then, and fall
To make paiment, while I call.
Ponder this, when I am gone ;
By the clock 'tis almost *One.*

TO KEEP A TRUE LENT.

*I*S this a Fast, to keep
　　　　The Larder leane ?
　　　　　　And cleane
From fat of Veales, and Sheep ?

Is it to quit the dish
　　　　Of Flesh, yet still
　　　　　　To fill
The platter high with Fish ?

Is it to fast an houre,
　　　　Or rag'd to go,
　　　　　　Or show
A down-cast look, and sowre ?
　　　　　　　　　　No :

184

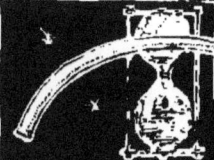

No : 'tis a Fast, to dole
>Thy sheaf of wheat,
>>And meat.
Unto the hungry Soule.

It is to fast from strife,
>From old debate,
>>And hate ;
To circumcise thy life.

To shew a heart grief-rent ;
>To sterve thy sin,
>>Not Bin ;
And that's to keep thy Lent.

CLOATHS FOR CONTINUANCE.

*T*HOSE Garments lasting evermore,
Are works of mercy to the poore,
Which neither Tettar, Time, or Moth
Shall fray that silke, or fret this cloth.

*T*O his Book's end this last line he'd have plac't
  Jocond his Muse was ; but his Life was chast.